How and Why Science

Science
at
Home

How and Why Science

Science at Home

World Book, Inc.

Chicago London Sydney Toronto

Acknowledgments

The publisher of Childcraft gratefully acknowledge the courtesy of illustrator John Sandford and the following photographers, agencies, and organizations for the illustrations in this volume. Credits should be read from left to right, top to bottom, on their respective pages. All illustrations are the exclusive property of the publisher of Childcraft unless names are marked with an asterisk (*).

  8-9 G.I. Bertnard/Oxford Scientific films from Animals Animals*
12-13 Archive Photos*; Leonard Ferrante, Tony Stone Images*; University of California, Davis*
24-25 Mel Lindstrom, Tony Stone Images*
28-29 Dan Rest

World Book, Inc.
525 West Monroe
Chicago, IL 60661

Editors: Sharon Nowakowski, Melissa Tucker
Art Director: Wilma Stevens
Illustrator: John Sandford
Cover Design: Susan Newman
Cover Illustration: Eileen Mueller Neill

Library of Congress Cataloging-in-Publication Data

Science at home.
     p. cm. -- (How and why science)
   Summary: Uses a number of simple experiments that can be done at home to explain such things as how soap bubbles can get really big, why glue sticks, and why paper towels are absorbent.
     ISBN 0-7166-7109-3
     1. Science--Experiments--Juvenile literature. 2. Science--Experiments--Methodology--Juvenile literature. [1. Science--Experiments. 2. Experiments.] I. World Book, Inc. II. Series.
Q164.S292   1998
507.8--dc21   98-6596

For information on other World Book products, call 1-800-255-1750, x2238, or visit us at our Web site at http://www.worldbook.com

Printed in Singapore

2 3 4 5 6 7 8 9 02 01 00 99

Introduction

Have you ever thought of yourself as a scientist? You may not have a laboratory equipped with a microscope, test tubes, beakers, or other fancy tools, but you can be a scientist in your own home! You can be a scientist in your kitchen. Open the refrigerator, look under the kitchen sink, and in the cabinets. You'll even find what you need in the bathroom! Are you ready to do **Science at Home?**

Science helps people answer questions such as, "How do soap bubbles get really big? Why does glue stick? Why do paper towels absorb spills?"

In this book, you'll meet Connor, and his Uncle Dan and Aunt Judith. Uncle Dan teaches chemistry in high school, and he has lots to teach Connor and you. Aunt Judith is a scientist, too, and she helps Uncle Dan and Connor with some sticky problems. Science games, puzzles, riddles, and folklore add to the fun. Don't worry about not understanding unfamiliar words—they are defined in the margins. The **Aha!** features and the **Breakthroughs!** highlight surprising science facts. When you are ready to try your skills, check out the **In Your Lab** sections.

Science is not just for professional astronomers, biologists, and chemists. Science helps all of us understand the world around us. Your home is a great place to start exploring.

Bubble Science

Chemistry is the study of substances and the ways they can be changed or combined.

Connor enjoyed visits at his Uncle Dan's house. Uncle Dan taught chemistry in high school, so he always had a way of turning chores into science experiments. As Uncle Dan stood at the kitchen sink putting detergent in the dishwater, Connor watched it foam and grow into mounds of sparkling suds.

"The suds remind me a little of shaving cream," said Connor. "Where do all these suds come from?"

"That's a good question," said Uncle Dan. "Suds are really just a lot of bubbles stuck together. But we can learn a lot from bubbles."

"Such as what causes them?" asked Connor.

"That's a start," said Uncle Dan. "To understand bubbles, we need to understand a property of water called *surface tension*. You see, water is made up of molecules. These water molecules are attracted to one another almost like iron to a magnet. And, because all the molecules are pulling on one another, the water stays together. This sticking together is called *cohesion* (koh HEE zhuhn)."

The water's surface tension keeps this pond skater from sinking.

The skin of a bubble is one of the thinnest things you can see with the naked eye. It would take thousands of bubble skins to equal the thickness of a human hair.

"Because of cohesion, the molecules at the surface of the water are attracted to the water molecules below and beside them rather than to the air above them. As a result, a sort of skin forms on the top of the water."

"A skin?"

"Well, it's not like your own skin. But it's a surface that takes some force to break. Have you ever noticed insects skating around on a pond?"

"Yes, I saw one at Crescent Lake last summer," replied Connor.

Uncle Dan continued. "Those insects are called water striders. They actually use the surface tension to walk on water."

"Cool," said Connor.

"Wait," said Uncle Dan, "I'll demonstrate surface tension." He got a small glass out of the cupboard and pulled a handful of pennies from his pocket. He filled the glass with water nearly all the way to the top and handed Connor the pennies. "Here, Connor. Carefully drop the pennies, one at a time, into the glass of water."

Connor dropped one, two, three, and more pennies in the glass. The water rose above the rim in a bulge. "Oh, I see," he said. "Surface tension keeps the water from spilling over the sides."

"Right," said Uncle Dan. "Surface tension and adhesion (ad HEE zhuhn). *Adhesion* is what holds water molecules to the rim of the glass."

I am skin without pimples
Or freckles or dimples.
Do I need to mention
That I'm S __ __ __ __ __ __
T __ __ __ __ __ __ ?

answer on page 32

9

"So where do bubbles come in?" Connor asked.

"Let's figure it out together," said Uncle Dan. "First, what shape are water drops?"

"Kind of round like a ball, I guess," answered Connor.

"Right. And what shape are bubbles?"

"Round, too," answered Connor.

"Right again. Surface tension makes all the water molecules pull toward each other. If no container is forcing the water into a shape, a small amount of water naturally takes a round shape." Uncle Dan ran water into another glass. "See how air bubbles form in the water? But when I turn off the water, most of the bubbles disappear. That's because surface tension pulls the bubbles apart and lets the air escape."

"But the sink with the detergent in it is still full of bubbles," said Connor.

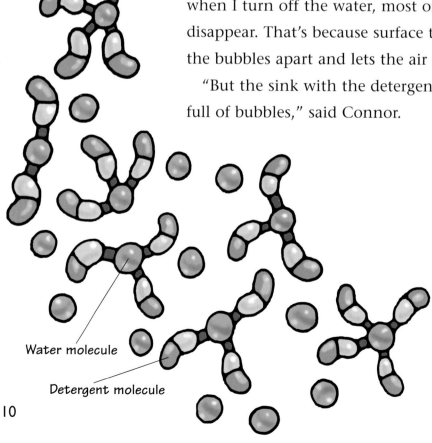

Water molecule

Detergent molecule

"You're one step ahead of me, as usual," said Uncle Dan. "Detergent has a special property. A molecule of detergent has one end that is attracted to water molecules and one end that is repelled by them. So detergent molecules wedge themselves between water molecules and push the water molecules apart. This is how detergent cleans your dishes. One end of the detergent molecule clings to dirt and the other to the water that washes the dirt away."

"This special property of detergent also weakens water surface tension and allows the surface of water to stretch more easily. The stretching allows bubbles to form better and grow bigger. Detergent also keeps water from evaporating. That's what makes soapy bubbles last longer."

"So a soap bubble is just a skin of detergent and water, with air inside," said Connor.

"Exactly!" Uncle Dan beamed. "How big do you think bubbles can grow? Let's find out."

Evaporation *is the process by which liquid turns into vapor. Wipe a shiny surface like a cool kettle with a damp cloth. Watch the water disappear. The water is now present in the air in the form of water vapor.*

Breakthroughs!

Some of the world's most famous scientists dabbled in bubble research. However, perhaps the world's greatest bubble researcher was Joseph A. Plateau of Belgium.

Plateau, born in 1801, recklessly threw himself into scientific research when he was a young man. To test an idea about human vision, he stared into the sun for up to 25 seconds at a time—something that is extremely harmful. As a result, Plateau gradually lost his eyesight. He became totally blind by his early forties.

1820's

1800

1873

Despite this setback, Plateau completed his most important work in his later years with the help of friends and family members who helped him study the way soap bubbles join. They examined thousands of groups of bubbles, measuring the angles their surfaces formed where they met. Plateau discovered something fascinating: bubbles connect at one of two angles, either 109° or 120°. In 1873, he published a book on these findings, *Statique des Liquides*.

Joseph A. Plateau

Plateau's discovery led many mathematicians to study bubblelike surfaces. They wanted to prove that because of surface tension, water molecules cover as little area as necessary. A bubble has the same quality. During the 1930's, a team of American mathematicians produced the first mathematical proof that this is true.

1930's

NOW

1995

Americans Joel Hass and Roger Schlafly made another important bubble discovery. They found that a container shaped like a double bubble takes up less space than any other container used to hold two equal volumes of different liquids. The double-bubble shape could reduce the area needed for fuel tanks in rockets. Try making the shape with your bubbles at home!

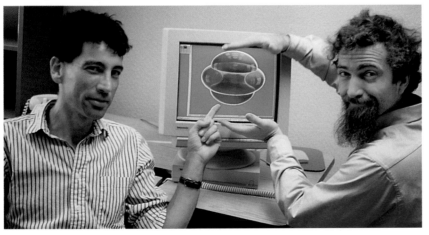

Joel Hass and Roger Schlafly

Breaking Tension

*Hmmmm . . . I wonder . . .
How can I see surface tension in action?
How strong is it?*

GATHER TOOLS

- 6 small bowls of water
- 2 needles
- 2 paper clips
- 2 pieces of aluminum foil, cut in 1-inch (2.5-cm) squares
- small pieces of facial tissue or toilet paper
- liquid soap
- toothpicks

Set up and give it a try

1 Carefully wash, rinse, and dry all of the bowls, needles, and paper clips.

Rub a needle between your fingers to make its surface a little oily. Place a piece of tissue *carefully* on the surface of the water in one of the bowls. Right away, drop the needle *gently* on the tissue. The paper will soak up the water and sink, but the needle will float.

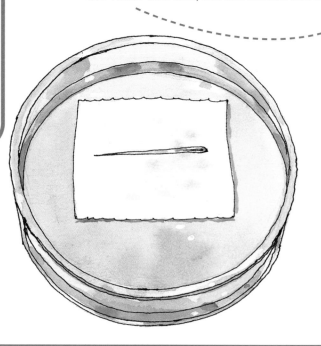

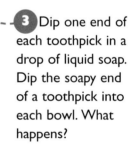

2 Use more tissue to *gently* float the paper clip on the water surface in another bowl. Float the foil square by itself in the last bowl.

Set up a control

Set up three more bowls with the same materials. Use the clean ends of the toothpicks.

3 Dip one end of each toothpick in a drop of liquid soap. Dip the soapy end of a toothpick into each bowl. What happens?

Try it again and again

- Use different amounts of soap.
- Use different kinds of soap—for example, chips from a bar of soap or grains of laundry detergent.

Now, write it down

Jot down your observations. Note what you did to each bowl of water and the item in it. How strong would you say surface tension is? What does it take to weaken surface tension?

Compare your notes with those on page 32.

Sticky
Situations

Uncle Dan and Connor were sitting at the kitchen table when the door opened and in walked Aunt Judith. She sat down at the table holding her umbrella.

"Uncle Dan has been teaching me all kinds of interesting things about bubbles. What happened to your umbrella?" Connor asked.

"I slammed the handle in the car door," Aunt Judith replied. "I hope I can repair it."

"Let's try the superglue," suggested Uncle Dan, opening the drawer. "Hey, why don't you tell Connor about adhesives, Judith?"

"Yeah!" said Connor. Aunt Judith was a scientist, too. She worked for a company that made plastics.

"Well, Connor, *adhesives* are substances, such as glue, paste, and tape, that we use to stick one thing to another," said Aunt Judith. "They work because of two related forces—*cohesion* and *adhesion*."

"I know what those are," Connor said. "Cohesion is the force that holds a substance together, and adhesion is the force that holds a substance to something else."

"Very good!" said Aunt Judith. "And what makes this glue adhesive so useful is that it starts out as a liquid. A liquid has less cohesion than a solid, so we can spread it on things in a nice thin layer. But more important, when an adhesive is in liquid form, its molecules can get very close to a surface. In fact, these molecules *bond* (attach) to the molecules of the surface. Now, what's the name of the force that makes things want to stick to other things?"

AHA!

Why doesn't superglue stick to its own container? Because there's no moisture inside the tube! Superglue needs moisture to stick. Your skin has moisture on it, so it's a perfect surface for bonding with superglue. Be careful when you use this glue—don't get stuck on yourself!

SUPER GLUE

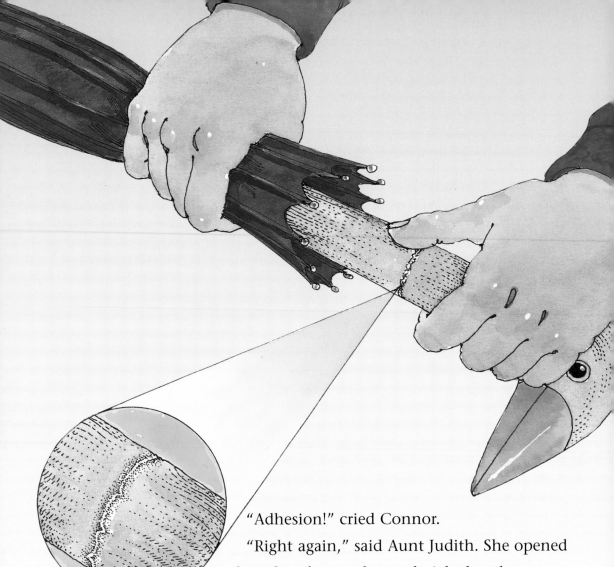

Glue is an adhesive.
It can bond things
together because of
adhesion and cohesion.

"Adhesion!" cried Connor.

"Right again," said Aunt Judith. She opened the tube of superglue and picked up her umbrella. "As I spread the superglue, it begins to bond with my umbrella handle. Then, when I attach the piece that broke off, the adhesive forms a bond with that surface. When the adhesive dries, its own molecules link together, forming a hard film with very strong cohesion. Then my umbrella will be fixed!"

"Fixed forever?" Connor asked.

"It should be. Some adhesives are so strong that it's easier to break the thing you've repaired than to break the adhesive bond."

"Are all adhesives that strong?" asked Connor.

"Not all of them," replied Aunt Judith. She picked up a pad of sticky notes. "The adhesive on these is designed to be just a little bit sticky. The notes stick only for a short time. And you can easily pull them off."

"Pretty neat," said Connor.

"Oh, and here's another kind of adhesive." She waved a roll of stamps. "Stamps and envelopes have a special kind of adhesive called *gum*. Unlike superglue, you can make gum sticky again and again. After it dries, just moisten it. Then you can peel it and restick it. Gum forms a bond strong enough to fasten paper. If you've ever steamed open an envelope

I'm sticky when you lick me,
I dry out when you stick me.
I help your letters come.
You can't chew me up,
but I'm G ___ ___

answer on page 32

and then sealed it back up, you've seen gum in action!"

"We made paste from flour and water at school once," said Connor.

"Yes," said Aunt Judith. "Flour is a type of starch. Mixing starch with water makes a sticky paste. Starches are good adhesives because their molecules can attach to other things."

"Our teacher once told us that glue was made from boiled animals."

"Yes, that's true. We use the word *glue* for all kinds of adhesives. But only adhesives made from animal parts are really glue," replied Aunt Judith. "When skins and bones are boiled, they

release a protein called gelatin. It's the same stuff that gelatin desserts are made of. Gelatin is naturally sticky. Glue makers dry the gelatin, crush it into powder, and add other ingredients. You have to add water before you use it. Other adhesives are made from artificial products such as nylon, which is a type of plastic."

"Look at all of the things around here that use adhesives," called Uncle Dan with his arms full.

Soon, Connor and Aunt Judith found themselves in a sticky situation as they explored the pile of tape, bows, bandages, note paper, stamps, and other sticky things.

AHA!

The rubber tree is the source of a natural adhesive called *latex* (LAY tehks). The tree has its own use for this substance. When a hungry insect chomps on a rubber tree leaf, it gets a sticky mouthful. Unable to chew, the insect has its last meal!

Your Own Super-Adhesive

Hmmmm . . . I wonder . . .
Can I make my own super-adhesive?
Can I make it from common
substances we have around the
house?

GATHER TOOLS

- disposable cups
- measuring cup
- measuring spoons
- teaspoon
- coffee filters
- milk
- white vinegar
- baking soda
- rubber bands
- test materials such as jars, pencils, paper clips, toothpicks, rubber bands, and papers

Set up and give it a try

1 Pour 1/2 cup (118 ml) milk into one of the disposable cups. Add 1 tablespoon (14.5 ml) of vinegar to the milk and stir. For best results, use clean utensils.

2 Place a filter in a cup. Use a rubber band to hold it in place. Pour the milk mixture into the filter. Let it drain for half an hour, or until the solids are as dry as you can get them. (Drain twice if necessary.)

3 Throw away the liquid that runs out of the milk mixture. Then put the solids in the cup. Rub the solids between your fingers. Would they make a good adhesive?

5 Test this glue for adhesion on your test materials. (Get permission to use the items.) How well does it work? On paper, is it as strong as the glue on an envelope or more like a sticky note?

4 Add a teaspoon (5 ml) of baking soda to the remaining solids. Stir well. Cover the mixture and let it sit for 24 hours.

6 Is the glue waterproof?

Try it again and again

• Use heavy cream instead of milk and lemon juice instead of vinegar.
• Try replacing the baking soda with other substances, such as detergent, milk of magnesia, or crushed-up chewable antacid tablets (ask for permission first).

Set up a control

If you want to know whether more of one ingredient—such as vinegar or milk—makes your glue stronger, divide a batch into three clumps. Add a little more vinegar or milk to one clump, a lot more to another clump, and none to the third. Compare the glues.

Now, write it down

Jot down the exact recipes you used and describe the type of glue each one made. Note which recipes worked best on which substances—for example, on paper, wood, plastic. Which ingredients made the best glue? Why do you think that is?

Compare your notes with those on page 32.

An Absorbing Tale

Connor had a question for Aunt Judith the next time he visited her.

"Aunt Judith, last night Dad gave Mom some carnations—you know, those frilly flowers. Some of them were green. I had never seen a green flower, but Mom said they were dyed. When I looked at them, I could see that the dye was inside the flower! How can this be?"

"The answer is related to something you've already learned about," replied Aunt Judith. "Remember the word *adhesion?*"

"It's the way things stick to other things," said Connor.

"Yes, and cohesion is the way things hold together themselves," continued Aunt Judith. "Well, adhesion and cohesion can be pretty powerful forces."

"That's really interesting. But I still don't understand how my mom's carnations turned green," said Connor.

"I'm getting to that," replied Aunt Judith. "A plant's stem has tiny tubes called *capillaries* (KAP uh lehr eez). When water enters a capillary, its molecules are more attracted to the walls than to each other. This attraction, called *capillarity*, lifts the water upward against gravity. Capillarity is how water climbs from roots deep underground to the tops of the tallest trees."

Water travels up a plant stem through these tiny tubes called capillaries.

White carnations dyed blue

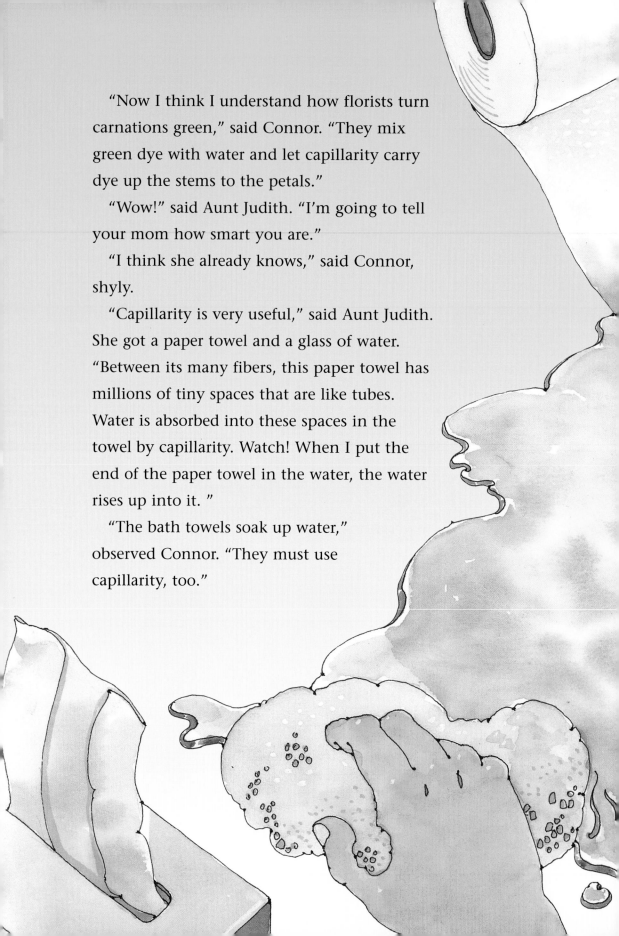

"Now I think I understand how florists turn carnations green," said Connor. "They mix green dye with water and let capillarity carry dye up the stems to the petals."

"Wow!" said Aunt Judith. "I'm going to tell your mom how smart you are."

"I think she already knows," said Connor, shyly.

"Capillarity is very useful," said Aunt Judith. She got a paper towel and a glass of water. "Between its many fibers, this paper towel has millions of tiny spaces that are like tubes. Water is absorbed into these spaces in the towel by capillarity. Watch! When I put the end of the paper towel in the water, the water rises up into it. "

"The bath towels soak up water," observed Connor. "They must use capillarity, too."

In a tube tinier than a hair,
Water climbs up without a stair.
An amazing feat in all clarity,
I'm talking about
C __ __ __ __ __ __ __ __ __.

answer on page 32

"Yes, and so do facial tissues and some kinds of clothing. When we need to take up moisture, we use these absorbent materials. Capillarity lifts water up a tube until it can't lift the weight of any more water. In a larger tube, the water cannot climb as high because the larger amount of water weighs much more. That is why capillarity occurs in small tubes,

AHA!

Why are cotton clothes comfortable to wear on hot summer days? Cotton fibers are long, hollow tubes. On a hot day, the cotton fibers in your shirt and shorts quickly draw sweat away from your skin, keeping you comfortable.

Which are more absorbent, the tan colored, unusually shaped natural sponges, or the artificial sponges that are colorful and rectangular? Test for yourself the next time you wash the car or take a bath.

where the weight of the water is smaller, and the water can be lifted higher."

"Do other things have capillaries?" asked Connor.

"For centuries," Aunt Judith continued, "people have used sea animals called sponges for bathing and cleaning. Sponges have soft skeletons made of an absorbent material called *spongin* (SPUHNJ ihn). Spongin is full of tiny tubelike spaces."

"Do you mean that the sponges we use to clean our car were sea creatures?" asked Connor.

"Your sponges are probably not natural ones," said Aunt Judith. "Most of the sponges we use

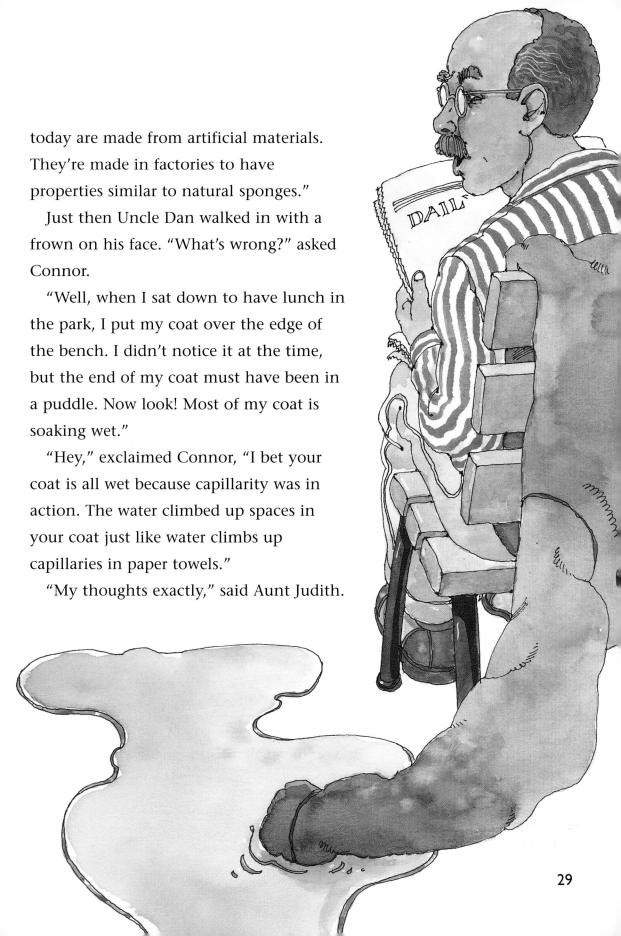

today are made from artificial materials. They're made in factories to have properties similar to natural sponges."

Just then Uncle Dan walked in with a frown on his face. "What's wrong?" asked Connor.

"Well, when I sat down to have lunch in the park, I put my coat over the edge of the bench. I didn't notice it at the time, but the end of my coat must have been in a puddle. Now look! Most of my coat is soaking wet."

"Hey," exclaimed Connor, "I bet your coat is all wet because capillarity was in action. The water climbed up spaces in your coat just like water climbs up capillaries in paper towels."

"My thoughts exactly," said Aunt Judith.

29

Capillarity

Hmmmm . . . I wonder . . .
How fast can molecules climb
through capillaries?
How much work can they really do?

GATHER TOOLS

- paper towels
- facial tissues
- paper napkins
- toilet paper
- 4 small, clear glasses or jars
- food coloring
- a spoon
- water

Set up and give it a try

1 Fill each glass one-fourth with water.

2 Add a few drops of food coloring to each glass and stir.

3 Fold each absorbent material into 4 layers. Put a folded material in each glass. Which do you think is most absorbent? least absorbent?

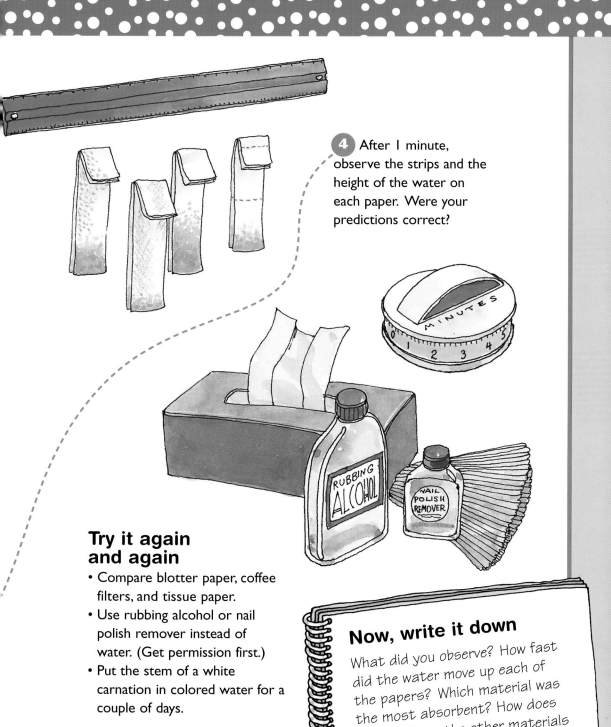

4 After 1 minute, observe the strips and the height of the water on each paper. Were your predictions correct?

Try it again and again

- Compare blotter paper, coffee filters, and tissue paper.
- Use rubbing alcohol or nail polish remover instead of water. (Get permission first.)
- Put the stem of a white carnation in colored water for a couple of days.

Now, write it down

What did you observe? How fast did the water move up each of the papers? Which material was the most absorbent? How does it differ from the other materials in the way it looks and feels?

Compare your notes with those on page 32.

Time To Think

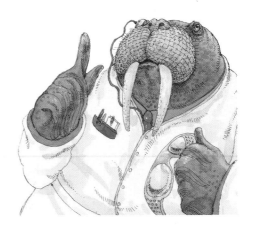

"The time has come," the Walrus said,
    "To talk of many things:
Of shoes—and ships—and sealing wax—
    Of cabbages—and kings—
And why the sea is boiling hot—
    And whether pigs have wings. . . ."

From *Through the Looking-Glass*
by Lewis Carroll

Answers & Lab Notes

Answers — Rhyming riddles

page 9: surface tension
page 19: gum
page 27: capillarity

Lab Notes

Here are some notes and findings you may have made when doing the labs presented in this book. There aren't any right or wrong notes. In fact, you probably made many observations different from the ones given here. That's okay. What can you conclude from them? If a lab didn't turn out the way you thought it would, that's okay too. Do you know why it didn't? If not, go back and find out. After doing a lab, did you come up with more questions, different from the ones you had when you started? If you did, good. Grab your journal and your science kit and start looking for more answers!

pages 14-15 *Breaking Tension*

Because of surface tension, the water acts as if a thin, elastic film covers its surface. Water's surface tension is extremely high compared to many other liquids. Water can support objects heavier than itself, such as a carefully placed needle. However, even a small amount of soap can reduce the water's surface tension and make the item sink. By doing the control, you know that it is the soap, not the toothpick, that reduces the surface tension.

pages 22-23 *Your Own Super-Adhesive*

At first, the milk solids do not feel at all sticky. When the baking soda is added, the mixture fizzes like soda pop. That is the baking soda reacting with the vinegar. When stirred, the solid material turns creamy white. It makes a good adhesive, especially on paper and wood.

pages 30-31 *Capillarity*

Some paper products, such as paper towels, are designed to soak up and hold water. However, others, such as coffee filters, are not. It should be no surprise then that a coffee filter would soak up water fast, but not hold a lot of water. Three cheers if you made this prediction before testing the materials.